DSC SPEED READS

COMMUNICATIONS

CW00553935

Meetings

Helen Rice & Maria Pemberton

DIRECTORY OF SOCIAL CHANGE

Published by
Directory of Social Change
24 Stephenson Way
London NW1 2DP
Tel. 08450 77 77 07; Fax 020 7391 4804
email publications@dsc.org.uk
www.dsc.org.uk
from whom further copies and a full books catalogue are available.

Directory of Social Change is a Registered Charity no. 800517

First published 2011

Copyright © Directory of Social Change 2011

ISBN 978 1 906294 25 0

British Library Cataloguing in Publication Data

A catalogue record for this book is available from the British Library

Cover and text designed by Kate Bass
Typeset by Marlinzo Services, Frome
Printed and bound by Martins the Printers, Berwick-upon-Tweed

All Directory of Social Change departments in London:
08450 77 77 07

Directory of Social Change Northern Office:
Research 0151 708 0136

For other titles in the DSC SPEED READ series go to:
www.dsc.org.uk/Publications/SpeedReadSeries

Contents

Introduction

'Meetings are indispensable when you don't want to do anything.'

John Kenneth Galbraith

Who will this book help?

At work we spend a lot of time in meetings. Sometimes we can wonder why we are there at all, as nothing seems to move forward as a result. Poorly conducted meetings are costly in terms of time, results and often goodwill. Running effective meetings is a skill. This book will be invaluable for new or existing chairs or minute takers wanting to develop their skills, or meeting participants who want to stop wasting time and make their meetings work for everyone.

What will it give you?

This book will give you a framework to run effective meetings. The guidelines are practical and include top tips to help you develop strategies to deal with difficult issues and people. It will help you be the very best you can be before, during and after meetings.

Chapter 1

What is a meeting?

Being clear about why you are holding a meeting is the first step to making it effective. This chapter looks at whether to call a meeting at all, and the key elements that will make it a productive occasion.

Defining a meeting

A meeting is any occasion when a group of people come together to share ideas and experiences. The size, composition, type and purpose of the meeting being held differ hugely between organisations and at different levels in organisations.

However, all meetings have certain elements in common: they involve people communicating with each other and exist for a purpose, even if not all the participants agree what that is. Broadly speaking, meetings are concerned with gathering and giving information, persuading, problem-solving and decision-making.

Do you need a meeting?

Meetings can become an end in themselves. Regular meetings – the monthly management meeting or weekly team meeting – can be held just because they

> **Top tip**
>
> Think about how you would achieve your objective without having a meeting. If it can be done without getting people into a room together, consider doing it. Meetings are expensive!
>
> **Cath Lee, CEO, Small Charities Coalition**

always have been. The first question you need to ask is whether a meeting is really necessary. If there is nothing meaningful to discuss, and no pressing issue to be resolved, you should consider cancelling it.

Sometimes regular meetings are held just so that people can update one another. Again, you should consider whether this is the best use of everyone's time, or whether written updates would suffice.

What makes a meeting effective?

There are a number of key areas that need to be in place for a meeting to be effective.

Checklist

- ❑ **Purpose of the meeting** – this must be clear and relevant to everyone involved.
- ❑ **Participants** – are the right people going to be present?
- ❑ **Agenda** – will it be an effective meeting tool?
- ❑ **The chair** – are they able to run the meeting effectively and enable all participants to contribute?
- ❑ **Minutes** – do you have the right sort of notes to promote action after the meeting?
- ❑ **Ground rules** – do you have a set of ground rules to help make the meeting work?

Ground rules, guidelines and terms of reference

Having a set of ground rules can:

- ■ provide a framework for behaviour standards
- ■ help all participants to feel safe
- ■ establish appropriate standards of confidentiality
- ■ help new participants to identify the group 'norms'
- ■ be referred to when there are instances of disagreement or conflict.

To be the most effective, ground rules require a sense of group ownership. Here are some suggestions:

- Actively listening to each other's ideas
- Welcoming appropriate humour
- Avoiding jargon
- Looking for the positive
- Being open and willing to learn from each other
- Challenging the opinion, not the person
- Confidentiality – the content of meetings and participants' personal views stay within the meeting (this would apply when discussing sensitive issues such as finances)
- Equal responsibility of all participants for the success of meetings
- No mobile phones or other interruptions
- Respecting each other's values and opinions, even if you don't agree with them
- Separating the person or personal from the issue
- Sharing your opinions and debating honestly
- Assuming that the views of all participants are equally important and valid
- Using language that respects and values diversity (age, gender, culture, sexuality, etc.)

It is important for your meetings that group members agree ground rules that are relevant to them.

For some meetings a separate set of guidelines or terms of reference can be useful (for example, subcommittees, advisory groups). These could include:

- information about the decision-making process – for example, whether decisions or recommendations made by a subcommittee must be ratified by another group, such as the management committee, board of trustees, etc.
- procedures for handling disagreement or conflict
- specification of how reports and presentations should be prepared and presented – for example, house style.

Top tip

Review the ground rules regularly – you could post them at the front of the room at the start of all meetings, to remind participants about the values and behaviours to which they have signed up.

Mike Phillips, Trainer and Consultant

Top tip

In the case of charities, the organisation's constitution, trust deed or memorandum of association will give specific details about how meetings should be held, usually called 'standing orders'.

Cath Lee, CEO, Small Charities Coalition

Chapter 2

Planning and preparation

A well-planned meeting has a greater chance of success than one that is called at short notice and poorly thought out. This chapter looks at all the necessary planning and preparation to be done before the meeting.

Purpose of the meeting

It is essential to think through what the purpose of the meeting is, and whether the purpose is going to be best achieved by holding the meeting. Many meetings are ineffective because they are not well thought through and these basic questions are not addressed.

As well as an overall purpose, it is likely that each item discussed will have a specific outcome to be met – this needs to be made explicit in the agenda. It will also inform who needs to be invited to the meeting.

The agenda: planning content

For any meeting to succeed, the participants need to have a good idea of what is going to be discussed and why they are there. Depending on the type of meeting, it is important to strike a balance between the level of formality and informality that you wish to create by having an agenda outlining the way that the meeting should proceed and who is responsible for what.

Including a 'Purpose and Objectives' section on the agenda can help to create a focus for the meeting's outcomes and keep everyone reminded of the main aim of the meeting.

In addition, think through the following points.

Subject matter

With regular meetings it is a good idea to ask the usual participants to submit agenda items in advance. Think about what topics need to be discussed and why, and be clear about whether an agenda item is for:

- information
- presentation
- ratification
- consultation
- decision (including agreeing actions)
- review
- discussion

and include it on the agenda.

Some meetings will restate their agreed ground rules at the beginning of each and every meeting. This is particularly useful if there are difficult individuals or issues being raised.

Avoid vague headings

Items on the agenda such as 'Any Other Business' and 'Matters Arising' can be the cause of lengthy, time-wasting discussions. 'Matters Arising' in particular can cause items that were discussed last time to be discussed again. If there are matters from the last meeting that need to be revisited, list them as separate items.

If you have asked for agenda items, there should be no need for the 'Any Other Business' item unless something very urgent arises – in which case, it should be first on the agenda anyway.

> **Top tip**
>
> Think about the purpose of the meeting in terms of outcomes. We might 'aim to talk about the fundraising event', but if we define the outcome as 'brainstorm ideas for fundraising event and explore the (dis)advantages of all', we will achieve more progress than simply pondering.
>
> **Ben Wittenberg, Director of Publishing, Policy and Research, DSC**

Top tip

It is better to send the participants reminders about reading minutes, taking action and bringing documents than to get there and have to waste time because people are not up to speed.

Jane Mumby, Programme Office Manager, British Film Institute

Avoid standing items that always appear on the agenda. Often this means that the person whose name is against this item feels that they must make a report, even if there is nothing meaningful to say. As a result, the most important items are squeezed time-wise. If standing items need to appear, make sure that you consider their place and importance in relation to other items.

Have a logical sequence and timings

Change the format of the agenda if necessary, so that items get the time and space they need. Take into account the urgency of the discussion required, and the time needed for each item. Try not to waste the first half of the meeting on the usual formalities and then run out of time for the really important issues.

Put timings against each item: this will ensure that you are not trying to cram too much in, and it will act as a guide to all the participants on how long each item is being given. An agenda in this format will help to keep things on track.

Case study

Training Services team meeting

Time	Subject	Lead
14:20	Update on projects – for information	
	■ information project	MT
	■ befriending project	AS
	■ service-user consultation project	JB
14:50	Update on launch event budget – for information	GM
15:05	Ideas for workshops at service user conference – discussion and decision on five workshops	JB

Domestic arrangements

The chair is usually responsible for calling the meeting, deciding who will be there and preparing the agenda; sometimes they will organise the domestic arrangements as well. Often for formal meetings there is a designated secretary, part of whose role will be to send out the agenda and papers and organise the domestic arrangements. In any event, the following points are worth mentioning here.

The meeting place

Make sure that this is comfortable, convenient and free from interruption. It is important that everyone at the meeting can see each other – a round or square table will help and is non-hierarchical. If you are chairing the meeting, ensure that you can see everyone even if you can't organise a round table – this means getting there first and positioning your seat in the right place.

Equipment

If someone is making a presentation, check that all the equipment is there and that the room is organised so that everyone will be able to see any slides that are being used.

Recording the meeting and note-taking

Every meeting needs to have someone appointed to take the notes, however brief. As a general rule of thumb, if decisions are being made, minutes should be taken. Do not attempt to chair and take notes at the same time, otherwise neither role can be carried out successfully. Depending on the meeting, sometimes it is better to have a non-participant taking the minutes so that they can concentrate solely on making an accurate record of what is going on, rather than trying to contribute as well. It also helps if the minute taker understands something about the subject matter.

Top tip

Make sure the agenda is sent out, with any accompanying papers, in good time for all the participants to read and consider the issues that are to be discussed. A good rule of thumb is to send everything out one week before the meeting.

Jane Mumby, Programme Office Manager, British Film Institute

Working with the minute taker

A short meeting between the chair and the minute taker before the main meeting can be helpful to sort out the following things.

Type of notes needed

There are many different types of meeting notes, from simple action points to full-blown minutes – so establish what type is needed before the meeting (see p. 21).

Technical terminology

The chair can outline and explain any technical terminology that may arise in the meeting.

Clarifying the discussion

The chair and minute taker can agree how to deal with any clarification that the minute taker might need during the meeting. For example, will it be acceptable to interrupt the meeting if the need arises?

Explain the structure of the meeting

If the minute taker is new to the particular topic area, this will help to give them a context to work in.

Agree deadlines

Agree the timescale for producing the draft minutes and the target date for circulating them to the participants.

Seating arrangements

Do not have the minute taker sitting in an unobtrusive corner away from the main group. It undermines their role and makes any necessary involvement difficult.

Where next?

Minute Takers' Handbook, P Ticher and L Comer, DSC, 2002.

Be supportive

To help ensure an effective meeting, the chair should be as supportive as possible towards the minute taker. Giving a summary at the end of each item will help the minute taker hugely. In many instances, this is all that is required in the minutes and this summary can be invaluable, especially if a complex technical issue has been discussed.

Case study

In one team, the members take it in turns to take minutes of their monthly meeting. This works well because it means that all the members have an equal chance to participate. The format of the minutes has been established so that everyone is clear how the notes need to be presented. The minute taker uses a laptop in the meeting so that the minutes are circulated almost immediately after the meeting ends. This has helped with people meeting their actions, as they cannot claim late-arrival of minutes as the reason for not having done what they agreed to do.

Chapter 3

Roles and responsibilities

Poorly chaired meetings can be demotivating for all concerned, but we also have responsibilities as meeting participants and minute takers. This section looks at the roles and skills needed to be an effective meeting chair, participant and minute taker.

Chairing the meeting: role and skills

The most obvious chair within a charitable organisation is that of the chair of the board of trustees, but of course many individuals within the organisation may need to become the chair of a meeting. Those chairing the meeting may change quite frequently, so the person having to chair may hold a more junior post than other participants, which in turn can bring its own challenges.

It is the chair's role to ensure that the meeting functions properly, everyone is able to contribute fully, all the agenda items are covered and all necessary decisions are made. The chair must provide leadership but not dominate the meeting: the role is one of facilitation and order.

Planning and preparation constitutes a large part of the chair's role. Thorough preparation is key to a successful meeting. As well as ensuring that the agenda is kept to, the chair should make sure that appropriate minutes and/or actions are recorded and appropriate follow-up is completed when necessary.

As mentioned previously, the chair needs to make sure that the purpose of the meeting is achieved and that members know what is expected of them as a result. However, this can be quite a challenge if problem situations or behaviour are involved. The skills of chairing a meeting can be learned and are particularly important in challenging situations.

Becoming an effective chair

Many of the skills of chairing meetings are used in other areas of our work and personal life; other skills you can practise and develop. Above all you need to think through the following areas.

Context

Know why the meeting is being held (its purpose) and what outcomes you wish to achieve. Understand the issues and topics to be discussed.

Participants

Have personal knowledge of the group or committee members. If difficult issues are to be discussed at the meeting, it can be useful to speak with essential participants beforehand to hear their perspectives and prepare for any difficult issues that may arise. The chair should always be aware of the needs of the group and should make every effort to include every individual in the discussion.

Timekeeping

Begin the meeting as close to the start time as possible – people's time is valuable. Always finish on time, if not before. Manage the timings around each agenda item to avoid overrunning.

Where next?

DSC runs a course on the skills of chairing meetings. See www.dsc.org.uk/chairingmeetings for more information.

Role

Be aware of your role as chair.

- How do the group or committee members perceive you?
- What do people expect from you as the chair?
- Did you call the meeting?

Ambience

Set a positive tone early in the meeting. Greet people before you sit down, and break the ice with some light humour to relax the group. People are often tentative and guarded during the first few minutes. Show the participants that you are well prepared and are taking the meeting seriously: this helps to set the tone for a focused meeting.

Top tip

Provide refreshments, if appropriate, as people bond around food and drink.

Procedures

Know how things should be done – that is, know the standing orders (see top tip, p. 7). Ensure that any ground rules are being followed.

Active listening

Listening is the most essential skill of the chair. Ensure that all members in the meeting are listening to each other by not allowing splinter conversations to happen. Allow plenty of time for everyone to present different viewpoints. Give your opinion last so that you don't close down useful discussion.

Managing the discussion

Open the meeting by stating the purpose and objectives and outline the terms and scope of the discussion. Keep the discussion on track by restating the objective in order to remind participants of the topic and the goals of the meeting.

Questions

Using the right types of questions can help to make sure that there is maximum relevant participation. Here are some particular examples.

Open questions

These should be thought-provoking, specific and relevant. They should point the discussion in the right direction and begin with 'who', 'when', 'why', 'what', 'where' and 'how' questions to avoid 'yes' or 'no' responses. For example: 'When do we need to implement this?'

Overhead questions

These are wide and addressed to the whole group. This method has the advantage of avoiding the embarrassment of individual members who may be unprepared and unable to answer. It is useful also for starting a discussion and focusing the group. For example: 'What are people's views about seeking Lottery funding?'

Direct questions

These are questions directed at an individual. They can be used for a variety of purposes: to bring in a person with specialist knowledge, to bring someone new into the conversation, or to engage a talkative member to take the conversation forward when the pace is flagging. For example: 'Richard, tell us a bit more about your experience of legacy fundraising.'

Redirected questions

To avoid the meeting moving back and forth between two members, the question can be directed at someone new and can be used as a link to coordinate a number of points, thus ensuring continuity of ideas. For example: 'Kim, how do you think Mary's suggestion would work?'

Case study

Linda Mitchell, a consultant, coach and facilitator, rebalances the percentage of positive to negative comments in meetings. She starts every single meeting with a 'go round the room', where everyone is encouraged to say at least one positive thing about something they have achieved or that has happened at work or home, or that has made them feel good. It can be on any topic. She finds that this constructively positive start makes a real difference.

Relay questions

This is a question put to the chair that is relayed to a member for a reply. It is useful when the chair does not wish to give personal views, get involved in an argument or influence the conclusions of the group. For example: 'That's a good question. How did the rest of you deal with that problem?'

Reverse questions

The person posing the question is asked to answer it. This can be used to encourage someone to think again, or to bring someone's specialist knowledge to the fore. For example: 'I know you have lots of experience in this area, so can you tell us more about how you think it would work here?'

Closed questions

These are questions which can be answered only with a 'yes' or 'no'. They can be valuable when you are seeking agreement and/or wrapping up a topic.

Summarising

This can be very usefully used in a number of ways during and at the end of the meeting to:

- clarify where the discussion has reached and move it forward
- clear up any misunderstandings – if your summary as chair is inaccurate, it will provide participants with the opportunity to correct your own, and everyone else's, understanding
- refocus the discussion when it is getting off track
- tie up each point and move on to the next issue
- help the minute taker.

Agree the next meeting

At the end of the meeting agree or confirm the date, time and place of the next meeting. Thank everyone

Top tip

A final summary at the end of the meeting to reiterate key decision and actions will help to make sure that everyone knows what the next steps are, and will provide participants with a sense of what has been achieved.

Jane Mumby, Programme Office Manager, British Film Institute

for coming and for their contribution, and after the meeting, check the minutes with the minute taker before they are circulated.

Participating effectively in meetings

Checklist

- ❏ Arrive on time – it is infuriating to have to wait to start until everyone is there.
- ❏ Read papers that have been circulated. It is essential to be prepared and not try to catch up while the meeting is in progress.
- ❏ Listen to what other people have to say. Avoid interrupting and talking over people – try and catch the eye of the chair if you have something that you want to say and are having trouble interjecting.
- ❏ Give your views – if you have been invited to be there, presumably you have something useful to say, so say it. Try to avoid sitting in silence and challenging decisions after the meeting has finished.
- ❏ Think about how to present your case.

The following **SHARE** plan may help.

State   Be sure of the facts and your opinions, sum them up briefly and state your proposition.

Highlight   Present your best case by stating and highlighting your best reason for the proposition. Your argument's strength will depend on its quality not its length.

Anticipate   Consider all possible objections and anticipate your response. This will help you decide whether to contribute to the discussion, and will act as a check on the soundness of your reasoning.

Repeat   Always end with a repeat of the essence of your argument.

Where next?

'Essential Tips for Chairing Meetings' My DSC free download: tinyurl.com/ essentialtips

Where next?

A Chair's First 100 Days, NCVO, 2005.

Evidence Have instant examples and evidence ready in case anyone challenges your proposition. However, you should be careful not to slant the evidence to suit your case; others may see through this, so instead give a well-rounded response and viewpoint.

Taking responsibility

We all need to take responsibility for our own actions – it is not just the responsibility of the chair to deal with conflict. Conflict often occurs because of assumptions that we make, so it is important to be self-aware.

Dos and don'ts

Don't make your mind up on first impressions.

Do listen actively.

Don't stereotype.

Do be influenced by positives as well as negatives.

Don't be judgemental.

Do be aware that people will behave differently in different situations, as you do.

Effective listening followed by a considered response will always be the safest and most effective route to getting your view across. Similarly, when you are talking, be aware of how others are listening. Consider what are they seeing, hearing, feeling, remembering and associating, and what expectations they have. Good listeners are generally listened to because they help to build rapport.

Case study

One leadership team, fed up with 10 and 15-minute latecomers, decided to self-impose a fining system. £1 is paid for every minute late, with all monies going to a named charity at the end of the year. No one has ever been fined more than £5!

Minute taking: producing clear and effective notes

It is essential that minutes are produced, but how formal these are will depend on the type of meeting being held. Formal committees sometimes require detailed minutes, whereas more informal meetings may only produce a list of action points to be completed after the meeting.

Sometimes minutes are used as a communication tool to keep people who were not at the meeting up-to-date with what is going on. In this instance it may be necessary to record the threads of the discussion as well as actions. It is very unusual to have to produce verbatim notes or attribute particular points to named participants. However, sometimes participants may feel so strongly about a point that they wish the exact details of what they have said to be recorded. However, this is the exception rather than the rule.

Always agree with the chair on the type of minutes that are required before the meeting starts. Whatever type of minutes you produce, it is important that they are produced quickly, are accurate and show what actions are required and by whom.

There are two parts to producing minutes: taking the minutes and writing them up.

Taking the minutes

Checklist

❏ Listen carefully to the discussion and watch the chair for specific sections of the discussion that need to be noted in a particular way. Listen for the chair's summaries for guidance.

❏ Take brief, relevant notes – this is more important than pages of irrelevant ones. Leave space between

Where next?

DSC runs a course on minute taking skills. See www.dsc.org.uk/minutetaking for more information.

Top tip

Ask the chair to summarise if you are finding it difficult to follow the discussion.

21

each item in your notes, in case you have to return to certain items later in the meeting.

❑ Note actions – who is being tasked with each item, and by when it needs to be done.

❑ Check through your notes at the end of the meeting and if information is missing or vague, check with the relevant meeting participant.

Writing them up

Checklist

❑ Draft the minutes at the earliest possible time. Keep your notes until they have been approved, as you may need to revisit them.

❑ Always try to be concise and accurate.

❑ Make sure that action points are clear – who is accountable and by when.

❑ Minutes should follow the structure of the agenda.

❑ Ask the chair of the meeting to check the minutes before they are circulated.

❑ Try to circulate the minutes quickly so that participants have plenty of time to follow through on the actions.

❑ Minutes from certain meetings may need to be signed by the chair as an accurate record of the meeting. This is usually done at the start of the next meeting after the participants have had the opportunity to have any amendments noted. Amendments should be written in and initialled by the chair, and recorded in the next minutes.

Top tip

Put an action column on the right-hand side of the minutes – include the initials of the person with the action, and the date when it is to be completed.

Ben Wittenberg, Director of Publishing, Policy and Research, DSC

Chapter 4

Challenging characteristics and situations

This chapter looks at how meetings can be problematic to manage. It outlines the types of challenging behaviour and situations, and gives techniques to help deal with them.

Even with the best plan in the world, meetings can still become difficult to manage. Discussions go off track, individuals try and take over the meeting, and sometimes it is just difficult to get to a satisfactory resolution of an issue. Participants get hot under the collar if the topic is contentious. Individuals dominate with their views, while others remain stubbornly silent.

Challenging characteristics

As with the rest of life, the participants at any meeting will have their own personalities, prejudices, opinions and agendas that they will bring along with them.

Sometimes the chair will have to find ways to manage particular types of character. Overleaf are some examples of challenging characteristics and how to manage them.

Case study

The manager of an educational charity realised that seating in meetings can make a huge difference to a meeting's outcome. Consequently, she makes a point of sitting next to a particular colleague in meetings: when they sit opposite each other they almost always argue, which does not help the meeting progress at all.

The aggressive shark

The shark is aggressive and dominant, ignoring the point in hand to have their say. Sit them next to you, so that you can nod easily to acknowledge their point or ask them to let others speak. Move on quickly from negative behaviour, keep cool while asking them to back down, and include and thank them when they show positive and constructive behaviour.

The wise owl

Keen and enthusiastic, the owl is well prepared and organised. They are intelligent, but may talk too much. A skillful way of interrupting them is by taking up one of their statements. If one member of the meeting has too much airtime this may upset other members, so make it clear that everyone will have their say.

The elephant who never forgets

The elephant has been around forever – they know everything about everyone and everything that has happened. They may be resistant to new ideas, or respond with: 'We tried that before, and it didn't work.' Value their time served by asking them to make positive suggestions about what might make it better and how you could improve on previous efforts.

The tiger who knows it all

The tiger is keen and can be a very useful character. The chair can ask the tiger to elaborate on issues about which the tiger is knowledgeable and which others in the meeting need to understand. However, tigers can take over and need to be kept in check. Therefore, having included the tiger where relevant to the meeting, they should be asked to listen to others' contributions. Asking others what they think of the tiger's contributions can also be useful in getting the tiger to clarify their own thinking.

Top tip

Always try to find the quickest ways of dealing with difficult behaviour – too much time spent on an individual means the meeting is less beneficial for the group as a whole.

Mike Phillips, Trainer and Consultant

The chattering chimp

Talking too much, the chimp often strays from the point and takes the conversation off on a tangent. It is important to bring the conversation back to the point up for discussion, so a simple 'That is really interesting – can we pick up on that at another time?' should work. At this point, quickly ask a question of another team member and move the conversation on in a productive way.

The timid mouse

Shy and retiring, the mouse should be made to feel important in front of the other participants. Ask them direct questions that are within their comfort zone and that you are sure they will be able to answer. Give them encouragement, as they may grow in confidence.

The sulky sloth

Generally unhappy and demotivated, the sloth cannot muster enthusiasm to contribute. The chair needs to make specific requests, demonstrating how their input will benefit the discussion. Draw out their knowledge and experience – perhaps when specific relevant topics arise – and provide an opportunity for the group to accept the sloth's views. This will also help the sloth to listen to others offering ideas.

The lazy hippo

Not interested in anything, the hippo does not want to be there. In fact they are quite happy for everyone to know they do not want to be there! They are incapable of adopting someone else's ideas. Try and move the conversation around to an area of their work, or to something that they are interested in when appropriate, as this may help to engage them.

Top tip

If people are talking among themselves when they shouldn't be, say: 'There are lots of little meetings going on at the moment, may we have just one meeting?'

Top tip

As a chair, you can try your best to avoid apathetic or disinterested participants by making sure that everyone is clear about their role and what is expected of them during the meeting.

The stiff-necked giraffe

The giraffe watches the others talking and generally feels superior to them. Treat the giraffe with respect and show that you are grateful for their input. Ask for their opinion when appropriate – they are generally sensitive and easily offended.

The slippery snake

Where next?

Meeting Together, L Graessle and G Gawlinski, Planning Together Associates, 2006.

Often smarmy and charming, the snake's speciality is red herrings and slippery banana skins. They are adept at slipping out of difficult situations, so avoid tackling them head on – stay cool and consistent, asking other group members what they think of the snake's views, comments and suggestions. Keep your wits about you and redirect questions and challenges to your advantage.

Challenging behaviour

Taking time to think about how you will deal with specific scenarios before a meeting can be extremely useful. Consider how you could deal with the following examples of challenging behaviour from meeting participants:

- consistently arrives late
- consistently leaves before the end of the meeting
- engages in side conversations
- introduces a personal problem or concern inappropriately
- monopolises the discussion
- is negative about everything, including other people's suggestions and ideas
- makes overlong contributions – goes on too much
- rushes the team to make a decision
- sidetracks – comments are way off subject
- remains silent – does not take part in the discussions

- snipes and argues with other participants
- partakes in and/or provides too much or inappropriate humour.

Fortunately, not all meeting participants behave like this, but forewarned is forearmed – so be prepared.

Problem situations

Having clear ground rules can help to make sure that things don't get out of hand. However, if there are disagreements, the chair needs to deal with them, even if this means being quite directive to bring things back on track.

The following situations are those that can typically arise, and need to be managed appropriately.

Unpopular decisions

When unpopular decisions need to be made, the chair may be under attack from individuals or the whole group. The chair must be prepared to present the case, acknowledge the weaknesses, anticipate the objections and emphasise the positive elements. When presenting to the group it is useful in these situations to acknowledge different communication styles.

- **Action-orientated people** would rather get straight to the point and focus on actions.
- **Ideas-led people** would rather hear something new and exciting.
- **Feelings-led people** want to know how people will be affected.
- **Facts-led people** like to hear logical and factual evidence.

Often all types of people will be present, so it is important to cater for a little of each. The information may still be difficult, but at least it might become a little more palatable. For example:

Top tip

Remember that there are a lot of people in the room and the majority of them will not be 'problem people'. Acknowledge these people frequently and always try to learn from them. Focus on rewarding and modelling positive behaviour: the carrot is better than the stick.

Mike Phillips, Trainer and Consultant

Top tip

It is useful to have an agreed procedure for argument or conflict resolution. Suggesting a 'timeout' – a short break in which participants can cool off when things become too heated – can bring back the meeting to a more calm and productive dynamic.

Top tip

If it is appropriate, try to speak to those who are obvious opponents in advance so that you can explain things at more length.

Cath Lee, CEO, Small Charities Coalition

Where next?

DSC runs a course on facilitation skills. To find out more, go to: www.dsc.org.uk/ facilitationskills

We are going to implement a new database system. I know that this will be quite disruptive for a while, but, as our research showed, this new system will allow us to be more efficient than before. We will be able to serve our beneficiaries better and it will present opportunities for new services in the future due to the extra data we will be able to produce. We have ensured that the staff will have enough external support to implement the system to make the transition as smooth as possible. This system upgrade is due to start next week.

Bad news

Sometimes bad news has to be given. If it is causing conflict, it may help to take a break and talk to those most concerned on a one-to-one basis. There may be legitimate reasons for their concerns that need to be explored.

In more formal meetings contentious issues may need to be voted on formally, and normally the chair's vote will act as the casting vote if there is a tie. In this case, there should be ample time provided for discussion of all the relevant points before the vote is taken.

Status differences

Sometimes meetings may include senior and junior members of staff. The chair needs to protect and encourage the junior members of the group. It can be a good idea to ask for their views first, as they may feel that they have to agree with more senior team members if these members' views are sought first.

Chapter 5

Getting win-win at meetings

Meetings regularly involve the need to influence and persuade others, whether you are a participant or chairing the meeting. You can find yourself negotiating results too. This chapter looks at how to approach these situations and the skills needed to succeed.

It is often a sign of a healthy and robust group dynamic when individuals can challenge and disagree with each other. It helps to avoid 'group think', collusion and apathy.

Influencing and persuasion

From time to time you may need to present an argument, either for or against something, in your role at a meeting. Here are some important points to consider when trying to influence or persuade people to your viewpoint.

Protect your rapport

Remember the importance and benefits of having an ongoing, healthy relationship with group members. No matter what the point or principle is at stake, a

Where next?

For a comprehensive manual on all aspects of negotiation, see: *Win Win*, ACEVO, 2007

group in permanent conflict is unlikely to be at its most productive, and ruined relationships are difficult to recover.

Stay neutral

Avoid taking positions – during discussions new information and insights can come to light. Keep an open mind and be prepared to be flexible. No one benefits from stubbornness.

Be prepared

Be as informed as you can when presenting or challenging points. Even when you have the facts, acknowledge that you may not have them all.

Get to know people

Build rapport with people outside the meeting time. Get to know them: what makes them tick, what needs and concerns they may have and the views and ideas that you share or disagree about.

Speak up

There is no benefit in muttering to yourself or others about something you wish would change. Make a request to the chair or group in a positive spirit.

Focus on the action, not the person

Don't take it personally and don't make it personal. Stay focused on actions and solutions and never make personal comments about a person's character.

Vary your pitch

Try to present arguments that will appeal to a range of preferences. Some may like to hear the statistics and facts which back up a proposition, while others may prefer to know the human or emotional impact of your suggestion. Some may be more interested in the result, while others will want to hear about how new or creative the proposition is. Pitch your argument to have maximum appeal, in order to maximise support.

Put yourself in others' shoes

Acknowledge other people's positions, needs, feelings, experience, knowledge, challenges and concerns. Try to see things from their point of view, and seek solutions that support a collaborative approach rather than a win/lose outcome.

Negotiating effectively

Sometimes within a meeting you will have to negotiate: this can range from formal negotiation over the terms and conditions of a grant or contract to internal resources and how they are utilised. Whatever the negotiation taking place, the following points are useful to consider.

Dos and don'ts

Do know your **LIM**its – **L**ike to have (ideal), **I**ntend to have (target), **M**ust have (minimum).

Do remember that what you see is always the top of the iceberg, and in order to negotiate, you need to find out about the hidden part of the iceberg – so 'seek first to understand, then to be understood'.

Do balance the talking with the listening – listen first, talk second.

Do think when and how: the way in which and the time when a negotiation is approached have more influence on the outcomes than all the other strategies combined.

> **Where next?**
>
> DSC runs a course on negotiation skills. For more information see www.dsc.org.uk/negotiation

Do have a BATNA (Best Alternative To a Negotiated Agreement) before getting into the negotiation process.

Do adapt your style to the other negotiators.

Don't see negotiation as a conflict, rather as an opportunity for a win-win scenario – keep the whole picture in your mind.

Don't highlight your shortcomings and don't hide obvious weaknesses.

We all have different styles of negotiation, but this collaborative model is the most common and most likely to achieve high-quality results.